CLIMBING ON COURSE

BERNIE MAY

MULTNOMAH PRESS
PORTLAND, OREGON 97266

D1591740

Illustrations by Joe DeVelasco
Design by Dannelle Pfeiffer

ISBN 0-930014-26-X
Library of Congress Catalog Card Number: 79-84717

CONTENTS

FOREWORD

I highly commend to you the writings of Bernie May, missionary jungle pilot and humble servant of God. Bernie brings to these pages an unusual ability to turn the aviator's commonplace into spiritually exciting lessons.

Whether or not you've ever flown, you'll find you've been there, too. As Bernie says, truth is for pilots and pilgrims alike. You will see yourself in these pages. Bernie's factual anecdotes, honest judgments and sensitive application of scriptural truth will make you chuckle delightfully, sigh over shared foibles, and nod with approval when he decides God knows best how to keep us climbing on course.

I have long been interested in the ministry of Jungle Aviation and Radio Service (JAARS) and the organization it serves, Wycliffe Bible Translators. These intrepid servants of God are quietly and carefully reaching the unreachable with the precious Word of God in some of the most remote areas of the globe. For many years Bernie has been part of that very effective team. It's from that background he shares—simply and effectively.

Read. Be blessed. And keep *Climbing On Course!*

Billy Graham

INTRODUCTION

Some time ago a BOAC jet came apart in a thunderstorm shortly after takeoff out of New Delhi, India. All the crew and the passengers were killed in the crash. The last words spoken by the captain before entering the fatal storm were, "We're climbing on course." When I heard about it I thought, What a great last position report—climbing on course.

"Position reports" are vital—for pilots and pilgrims. They indicate where we are at any given time. Whether I have learned more about flying from my moments with God—or more about God from my experiences in the air—I don't know. But I do know that as I have tracked the skies of this world—putting my confidence in instruments which have guided me through dark and rainy nights, or listening to a distant controller steering me to a final approach—God has taught me about faith, discipline and eternal values.

A lot of times I have been in what pilots call a "critical attitude." That means the aircraft is in danger of crashing because of its position in the air—nose high, one wing low, power off. That's me: nose high in pride, doctrinally off balance and spiritually powerless. It's a bad position report. But, more and more, as His Spirit takes the controls, I'm back climbing on course.

I share my experiences with you, hoping that you, too, will want to know Him better, and to learn with me what it means to "mount up with wings as eagles."

Climbing on course,
Bernie May

DEDICATION

To my wife, Nancy, who today completes 26 years as copilot.
Thanks for

> holding the light,
> checking the gauges,
> correcting my heading,
> caring for the passengers,
> and helping me hold it on course.

Bernie May
5 June 1979

ACKNOWLEDGMENT

God did a good thing when he put together as friends a pilot-sometime-writer (myself) with a writer-sometime-pilot. To Jamie Buckingham my sincere thanks for all his love, encouragement and editorial help.

THE MILLION DOLLAR SIMULATOR

The other day a lady asked if I had ever flown a jumbo jet—one of those huge birds that holds 400 passengers in its metal gullet. I almost said, "Yes," but had to limit my answer to, "Well, almost."

How do you almost fly a jumbo jet?

My good friend Roy Long, a senior pilot with a large commercial airline, is in charge of a jet pilot training program in Miami. Pilots preparing to fly the company's mammoth airships get their initial checkout in what is called a "simulator." It's an awesome-looking piece of machinery which contains a simulated jumbo-jet cockpit. Housed in a multi-million dollar training center, it stands on tall mechanical stilts which move a few feet back and forth—up and down—controlled by a roomful of computers.

One night Roy invited me to join him in a training session. While the regular pilots were taking a coffee break, he gestured toward the simulator.

"Strap yourself in the left seat, Bernie, and let's make a couple takeoffs and landings."

While I buckled up, Roy punched a few buttons on the console and somewhere a few rooms over, a metallic brain clicked and whirled in response and went right to work.

We found ourselves on the end of Runway 9-Left at Miami International. The computer left nothing to the imagination. I'd never been in such a high cockpit in my life. There was the Miami runway stretching out in front of me—glaring white in the mid-morning sun. I advanced throttle, heard the engines go from throaty rumble to mechanical scream, spooling up to max RPM. My jumbo started to roll forward as a stewardess somewhere back greeted the passengers. Beads of sweat formed on my brow while the runway flashed under me. The airspeed indicator crept past 140 KTS and Roy called out, "Rotate!"

I eased back the yoke. We were airborne—climbing into the hazy blue over Miami. In the weight of the controls, I could feel the huge craft behind me. *Sure would hate to land this bird in the Andes.* We climbed to pattern altitude. My copilot nodded as I circled the great field and lined up on final for the landing. Roy was calling out airspeed as I worked the throttles and controls—letting down for landing. I heard the wheels screech a protest on the runway and then felt the weight of the plane settle on the gear. My feet were on the brakes as I reversed the engines. We coasted to a shuddering halt.

"Not bad, Captain," Roy grinned. "Not bad at all for your very first landing in the L-1011." Running my sleeve across my brow, I was warmed by a feeling of accomplishment. No hitches or hang-ups. It felt good.

But it wasn't real. It was all a Disneyland make-believe. We hadn't traveled two feet. We never went higher than our stilts.

And that, I am slowly realizing, is a parable of much of our Christian experience. We build million-dollar simulators. We climb in, sing passionate hymns with an electronic organ that simulates 20 different instruments. We listen to exciting stories and even make emotional commitments. There's only one minor fraud. We never really take off. There is noise and motion—but we haven't gone anywhere.

"Spectator Christianity" has vaccinated us against the genuine article—participation Christianity. One church advertises, "For those who want more than a Sunday religion." Now, that's the way it should be.

Dr. Samuel Shoemaker asks us all, "What has Jesus Christ meant to you since 7:00 this morning? Is your Christianity ancient history or current events?"

God's invitation is to mount up with wings as eagles. Why be content with a simulator when you can fly?

HIDDEN WINGS

A friend of mine knows an airline captain who flies overseas routes for a U.S. carrier. Between trips to Europe and the Middle East, he runs a small filling station in the suburbs near his home. He gets a kick out of changing plugs and points and talking to the folks while he pumps gas.

One Saturday morning, dressed in his greasy overalls, he walked down to the local hardware store to pick up a wrench.

"What's new?" the store owner asked as he rang up the purchase.

"Ah, I'm thinking of taking the Cairo run this month," the captain said. "I enjoy flying to London and Frankfurt, but I think the change of pace will do me good."

He paid for the wrench and left.

Another customer, curious, asked, "Who's the world traveler?"

Rolling his eyes, the store owner nodded toward the departing pump jockey. "Some nut who runs the gas station down the street. Thinks he's an airline pilot!"

Both men got a good laugh out of that one.

It's easy to be deceived. I keep reminding myself of that when I see our JAARS people coming home on furlough. Arriving here at our JAARS Center in North Carolina, they look like ordinary people—a school teacher, a local farmer, an insurance salesman from Charlotte . . . or even a filling station operator. Who would dream that just a few days before, these same people were risking their lives flying a tiny airplane over the Amazon jungle, sending life-saving radio messages over the jigsaw islands of the Philippines, or rebuilding a damaged aircraft in the shadow of the Andes?

On the other hand, I was in the grocery store the other day, and this ordinary-looking young man kept telling me about his Father, the King.

You never know, do you?

BROKEN VOLUNTEERS

A stewardess was handing out pillows in the plush, first-class cabin of a transcontinental airliner. Pausing by a dignified lady in an aisle seat, the girl asked the passenger if she would like a pillow. The lady looked straight ahead, seemingly unaware of the stewardess.

The girl tried again—a little louder. **"Would you like a pillow, m'am?"**

No response.

After a long pause, the lady's husband leaned over and said, "I'm sorry, Miss, but my wife never speaks directly to servants."

Ouch!

Needless to say, the "stew" was a bit stewed. Most in that lofty occupation don't think of themselves as servants. Yet, in reality, that's exactly what they are. They exist to *serve* the passengers.

Unfortunately, the word "servant" is also unpopular among Christians. We chafe at an order to carry someone's load that first mile—let alone the second. And the idea of washing someone else's feet is only two points above repulsive.

Even among missionaries I find a cool response to this title—servant. The word "volunteer" seems to fit our image better. But God isn't looking for volunteers. To volunteer implies that we make the terms. Some of us have gone out, egos waving from our lances, to "do a great work for God." The fortunate ones come back broken, realizing God doesn't need volunteers. He's simply looking for a few good men and women who will report for duty. Servants.

If God's Word is going to be translated into every language in the world, it will only be accomplished through servants—servant translators, servant radio technicians, servant carpenters, servant pilots, servant secretaries. Servants who pray, servants who give, servant Christians everywhere.

And there's a bonus. Our Master talks directly to His servants. He even calls us friends.

PRACTICE MAKES PERMANENT

I never did like to play on the black keys. As a kid, it became such an issue to me that I quit piano lessons. I'd do it my own way. And for years, every time I sat down at the piano I played only on the "preferred" keys—the white ones. Finally, a few years back, I decided to take lessons again. After six months *my teacher* quit. It was no use. "My way" was so ingrained I could not break the old habit and do it correctly. The "black key syndrome" haunts me to this day.

It reminds me of something my colleague Merrill Piper says in his flight safety seminars. "Practice does not make perfect," says Merrill. *"Practice makes permanent."*

The principle has drifted back to bedevil our ministry again and again. Recently one of our pilots was practicing emergency power-off landings. We teach that this should be done with the engine idling. But this pilot shut if off completely. When the heavy plane began settling far more rapidly than expected , he attempted a quick restart. It didn't work. The plane crashed, injuring the pilot and damaging the aircraft.

"Where did he ever get the idea to kill the engine?" I asked Merrill as we reviewed the accident report. "He should have known better. Why did he do it?"

"Unfortunately," Merrill explained, "his instructors in basic training taught him to make practice landings that way. Even in advanced training this was accepted procedure. Later, they recognized that it was dangerous."

But the change came after our man graduated. When he got into one of our heavier planes, his old habit flipped a switch in his head and off went the power. His practice almost made *him* permanent.

I'm amazed at how hard it is to change attitudes and opinions that we learn early. I have friends who learned in their youth that the Sermon on the Mount was just for the Jews, or that miracles ceased after the first century.

I wonder how many of my classmates crashed because they didn't expect a miracle. Up came the old prejudice and off went the power. Or perhaps they haven't clung to the sure and changeless footholds of our Lord's timeless mountain message. But I have. The rock-firm promises have never given way beneath my trembling feet and searching hands.

Clinging to God's powerful promises . . . that's one practice our Lord makes perfect *and* permanent.

THE WORD OF A GAUGE

Jim Baptista is a detail man. Gripping a mental clipboard, he pores over every detail of pre-flight procedure before nosing his craft from terra firma.

One time I flew with him to Tucson, Arizona, to pick up a surplus DC-3 for JAARS. It looked like a good prospect and everything checked out as we took it down through the check list. Until we ran up the engines. Jim and I exchanged glances as a gauge showed the right-engine oil pressure was low. That's serious. We were certainly in no position to buy another engine so we did some checking.

The log book showed the engine was brand new. A further check showed the reason for changing the original engine was low oil pressure. It was rather difficult to accept that two engines, one of them new, could develop identical problems.

So the detail man decided to do a little experimenting. Crawling under the instrument panel, Jim reversed the lines on the oil gauges, attaching the right engine line to the left gauge and vice versa. You guessed it. Now the left engine showed low oil pressure. Conclusion: The gauge, not the engine, was at fault. Someone had installed a new, $12,000 engine because of a false reading on a $30 gauge.

For some reason, we habitually take the word of a gauge, simply because it appears before us on an instrument panel. A broken or malfunctioning oil pressure gauge, altimeter or compass could cause a pilot to take drastic action—action that might even cost him his life.

As we flew home, those two big engines purring on each wing, I thought of other gauges which proclaim "truth." Some call for radical change. Others assure me that everything's okay.

Call me a spiritual "detail man" if you wish, but I wonder about some

of those gauges. I've stopped taking the word of a gauge, even if it has always been right before. No gauge—no voice—gives a true reading all the time.

A gauge that's stuck in the green when the engine is going wild can be just as fatal as one that causes you to chop the throttle when nothing is wrong. The wise man reverses his lines now and then, checks the Manual . . . or even consults the Manufacturer.

Somewhere, sometime, it might save him a burn-out.

INSPECTIONS

Every time a member of Wycliffe is elected or appointed to a new position, he is required to undergo a doctrinal examination. So it wasn't much of a shock when a bulky envelope from the secretary of the board landed on my desk after I was elected to the board of directors. The politely worded note inside requested me to reaffirm my original doctrinal position.

That's okay. It gave me the opportunity to plunge into the Word and carve out restatements of what I believe about God, God's Son, the Holy Spirit, the Bible and other foundational truths.

About the same time I received a letter from my home church asking me to do the same for them. They've got a rule that all missionaries sponsored by the church should periodically be reviewed to make sure they haven't slipped into some form of false doctrine.

I joked with my wife that if I didn't know that the folks at Wycliffe and the officials in my home church loved me, I'd be feeling a little insecure with all these doctrinal examinations coming at me.

Inspections are a good thing. I've lived with them ever since I began in aviation. But as I penciled out the forms, I couldn't help thinking back to some things I'd been told about the aircraft inspections we conduct in our hangers at JAARS. We'd been giving our aircraft 100-hour inspections—a pretty sacred procedure among mechanics. But then someone got the idea to inspect our inspections. The results were painful. We found that our mechanics were spending a lot of time and energy inspecting the wrong things. We'd been extremely thorough—but thorough in the extreme.

Some parts were meticulously over-inspected while others went totally ignored. For instance, our crew religiously undid a hundred screws in the wing during each 100-hour inspection to look at the spar. *A spar wouldn't change in a hundred years of constant flight!* At the same time, we gave little or no attention to things like small rubber hoses or instrument air filters—things which deteriorate constantly and give us chronic problems.

We wore out our airplanes and mechanics with inspections, consuming time and energy on relatively unimportant matters while we blissfully ignored those items which needed our constant attention.

I don't mind inspections. But I get concerned when I'm checked for the wrong things. Not once has anyone checked me out on John 17, and how well I'm doing with Jesus' prayer "that they all might be one." At every investigation someone takes off my inspection plate and examines my wing spar of biblical inspiration, but no one ever checks my filters to find out if I'm so clogged up with unforgiveness and bitterness that love can't flow through. God has a different perspective...a different checklist. The Bible tells me that even if I leave everything behind, go off to some distant mission field, spend 60 years uttering doctrinally precise words—even giving my body to be burned and have not love....

Inspections are good. All of us need them.

If the right things get inspected.

By the right inspector.

I'm convinced the Master Designer who put us together is eager to maintain His high performance standards. If we'll only let Him.

GO, NO GO

Every airline has a "go, no go" list comprising a combination of weather factors, mechanical checklists and the pilot's own cockpit checklist.

Example: A malfunctioning instrument, a badly frayed seatbelt or a tornado at the end of the runway means a "no go." On the other hand, a burned out light bulb in the instrument panel, worn tires or just dirt and bugs on the windshield are acceptable problems; the pilot gets a "go"— he can take off.

When the chief pilots from all our overseas operations got together for a flight safety seminar, I began to realize that even "acceptable" problems can kindle a disaster if they are not handled correctly. When the pressure is on and the weather is bad, some small discrepancy hardly noticed on takeoff can loom suddenly like a vengeful giant. Just before a spectacular air-to-air collision, one airline pilot reported that there were so many bugs splattered on the windshield he could barely see through it. It was his last report.

We were just about through the safety session when one seasoned aviator spoke up and grounded us all.

"Frankly, gentlemen," he said, "it's not the discrepancies in the airplane that bother me as much as the discrepancies in the pilot. When I'm in the air with things inside me that I know aren't right—I become the hazard."

You won't find it in a pre-flight instruction manual—but he's right. Who wants to fly with a pilot who's just had a bitter argument with his wife. . .or who is seething underneath at his copilot. . .or who has an uncontrollable temper. . .or who is so filled with pride and self-righteousness that he refuses to listen to correction?

Bugs on the windshield. Nothing so urgent as a faulty fuel line or plunging oil pressure—just a little compromise with clear vision. Little things. Like petty jealousy, impatience, prejudice, careless words, prayerless mornings, impure thoughts. In an aircraft it's the little things which, in a crisis, could mean the difference between life or death. For the believer, bugs on the windshield could rob visibility at a critical moment of decision resulting in moral disaster or irreparable loss of witness.

Every Christian leader, pilot, parent or preacher needs to have his own personal "go, no go" list before he straps himself into a place of responsibility. When the going gets rough, everything better be up to specs.

CLEANING THE CONNECTIONS

It was a dark and stormy night. It really was. One of my closest friends is a professional writer who laughs at people like me who start a story that way. But when you're trying to make an instrument landing with a vintage DC-3 on an island in the West Indies with your ADF (automatic direction finder) out of whack—and it's a dark and stormy night—what else can you say? I can assure you it was no laughing matter.

That night as I approached Kingston, Jamaica, in a screaming gale, my ADF chose to rebel. It pointed straight ahead for a while. Then it pointed over toward Spain. At one point it aimed to the rear. Fortunately, I had dual ADFs on the plane; the second one remained loyal and I landed safely.

Later, I watched the radio repairman troubleshoot the faulty radio. After a few simple checks, he turned and said, "You'll never keep it on course with a bad connection, Captain. The problem is in this cannon plug." I watched as he disassembled the complicated plug with 20 pins which fit neatly into a 20-pin receptacle. Moisture in the connections had caused corrosion to build up on the contacts. The unwanted resistance in the wires resulted in an unreliable ADF.

Besides getting an instrument repaired, I got some good advice. "Every so often, Captain," he remarked, "you need to stop and clean up your connections."

The phrase repeated itself recently on an inner speaker when our family of five went on a vacation to the beach. There's nothing like five people in a crowded camper to test the condition of your wiring. At the end of the first day it was apparent that we had some fragile connections. The best communication we could manage was a lot of

harsh static. My wife threatened to go home. My oldest son, a high school senior, took courage in the fact that this would be his last family vacation. We couldn't even agree on what kind of soda pop to drink.

The next morning I decided we had to clean up some connections. We examined ourselves—each one in relation to the others. We found that parents aren't always fair and that resentments build up between brothers. We leveled with each other, confessed, prayed, cleaned up the connections and went on to have one of our best family vacations ever.

Now I'm thinking I need to check on some of my other connections. How about those with my fellow missionaries? Or my neighbors? Or my relatives?

If I'm going to stay on course and be effective in my work and ministry, I'm going to have to keep the connections clean—because for sure, there will be some more dark and stormy nights.

ON THE PROMISE OF A FRIEND

He said it so casually.

"Bern, how would you like to take a trip with me around the world?"

My businessman friend Bill Johnson and I had been strolling down a hot, crowded street in Quito, Ecuador.

"Are you serious?" I asked, astonished. I'd done a lot of flying over the jungles of South America but a flight around the globe was only daydream stuff.

"Sure I'm serious. I love to travel and have always wanted to go around the world. Why don't you come with me?"

It was a little overwhelming. Around the world! But missionaries are not, as a rule, wealthy. Such a trip would cost several thousand dollars, and besides, I suspected Bill's tastes were rather more sophisticated than mine.

We chatted on, plotting the details. We would visit Japan, Hong Kong, Taiwan, then our Wycliffe-JAARS program in the Philippines, down to New Guinea and Australia, up to Indonesia and over to Singapore. We would hit Southeast Asia and India, stopping at Tehran, Beirut and Rome before coming home. The trip would take six weeks and, I could tell from my friend's animated expression, would cost a small fortune.

Finally I spoke up. "Uh, Bill . . ." I stuttered, breaking into the conversation, "this really sounds great but . . . ."

Bill knew what I was thinking. Clapping me on the shoulder he said, "Now, Bern, don't worry about the expenses. I'll take care of everything—first class all the way!"

We hadn't even bought the tickets and I was already so excited I could hardly talk. I couldn't wait to get back home that evening and tell my wife. We talked into the night, thinking about all the mysterious, exotic places I would get to visit and explore.

However, that night as I lay my head on the pillow, a strange sense of conviction came over me. In the deep, quiet area of my life where God often speaks, I heard a silent voice.

"You're sure excited, aren't you, son?"

"Yeah, I guess I am."

There was a pause, then, "Do you realize why you are so excited, Bernie? It's because of the promise of a friend. The trip is still weeks away, but because you trust this man, you're acting as though it's already happened."

Another long pause. "How long has it been since you were that excited over My promises? Or . . . don't you trust Me as much as your friend Bill?"

I didn't sleep well that night. But the lesson was well-learned. And just as Bill's promise materialized and I was able to make that memorable journey, so I have discovered that all of God's promises are true. In fact, I can trust my Heavenly Father even more than the promises of all my friends.

Now that's something to get excited about!

OVERCONTROLLING

I can still hear my flight instructor of 20 years ago shouting above the engine noise of the Super Cub, "You're overcontrolling!"

He was right. As a beginning pilot, I was afraid if I didn't keep my feet firm on the rudder pedals and my fingers clenched tightly around the stick, the plane simply wouldn't stay in the air. I blush when I recall sitting in the cockpit, jaw muscles tight, stomach churning, flying all over the sky.

"Relax," my instructor grinned. "Ease off on the controls and the plane will fly itself."

That was good advice 20 years ago. It's even better advice today. The novice Christian develops ulcers because he's overcontrolling. The mature believer, however, has that relaxed look about him.

Even missionaries have discovered that it is possible to do the Lord's work without the Lord's power—but it will kill them in the process. However, when they let the source of power, the Holy Spirit, rule in their lives, they stop overcontrolling. White knuckles around the stick begin to relax. What used to be drudgery can become fun.

Those of us in JAARS have always had a certain pride in our professionalism. Yet our motto, "We do our best and the Lord does the rest," sometimes meant we thought we could handle most emergencies ourselves. If we couldn't, we would call on God.

Now many of us have come to realize that our best is not good enough. We used to throw around that phrase, "God is my copilot." No more. He's flying left seat—we are the copilot! The difference is, instead of giving God directions, we're taking orders from Him.

We find the power in the Spirit, not in our striving. Anyone can get uptight about tomorrow, and wander all over the sky today. The Spirit-filled man not only flies straight and level, but he's relaxed when he reaches his destination.

HOLDING PATTERN

The September heat marbled the air off the concrete apron as we taxied away from the terminal building in Richmond, Virginia. Jamie Buckingham, his lap full of charts, was beside me in the right seat. Bill Sasnett was in the rear, mopping his face with a handkerchief.

We were bound in our Helio Courier for New York City. Before leaving the terminal I had filed a flight plan with the FAA, requesting a direct route. In the jungle I feel comfortable flying the little Helio. But this was urban America, and at 120 mph I wanted to spend as little time as possible competing with jumbo jets around New York City.

Now, sitting at the end of the runway, I finished the run up. Mags, prop, generator, instruments—all okay. The cabin was like a furnace as we waited for our clearance. We wanted to hear those three sweet words, "Cleared as filed," and get on our way up and out of the heat.

Finally the radio crackled to life. "Helio Courier 242 Bravo, are you ready to copy your clearance?"

I could tell by the voice from the tower that we weren't going to get our direct route. Instead, we were directed to turn southeast after takeoff and climb to 3,000 feet—not the 7,000 I had requested. Then another controller gave us various headings which took us east toward Chesapeake Bay. We were then directed to climb to 5,000 feet, through turbulent air, zigzag over three different airways and finally head west. All this, to get us on the NYC airway which ran north.

It was aggravating, but the Air Traffic Control fellows have to take a lot of things into account. We weren't the only ones in the air. In fact, the NYC controller said he had 70 planes on his radar scope. Besides this, there were thunderheads which easily could have torn the wings off our plane.

We didn't get what we asked for. Instead, we got what was best for us—and best for everyone else, too.

Holding patterns, turbulent air, going east when you want to go north—all seem confusing. But when somebody who knows the way and the obstacles is plotting your path, you accept his instructions gladly.

Proverbs 14:12 tells us:

> *There is a way which seems right to a man.*
> *But its end is the way of death.*

The ways of God may seem to defy our reasoning. But He knows the end from the beginning. In the long run, God's skies are always friendly skies. Even when you're in a holding pattern.

LETTING THE PILOT PILOT

The wheels of the heavily loaded Cessna 206 had barely left the wet jungle airstrip. The pilot had the throttle pushed all the way to the firewall. He had done this many times before and was confident they would clear the huge trees.

Then, as nearly as we can tell, the passenger sitting next to him had a surge of panic. Glancing up, he saw the onrushing trees filling the windshield. Fearful they were going to crash, he tried to help. Apparently he took hold of the flight controls and pulled back. His assistance proved to be disastrous—almost fatal.

But his intentions were only the best. The fully loaded airplane wasn't climbing very rapidly in the hot jungle air. Huge trees at the end of the strip were looming large.

"My soul—what's wrong with that pilot? Is he asleep? Why doesn't he pull back on the controls?"

But it doesn't work that way. You have to build up airspeed before you point the nose skyward. Otherwise you'll stall.

The airplane pitched up, lost critical airspeed and began to settle toward the jungle below. The pilot wrenched the controls back and tried desperately to get the nose down. But it was too late. As the airplane reached stalling speed the heavy engine pulled the nose over sharply and the craft spun to earth.

By God's grace, no one was killed, but all were injured, the pilot most seriously. Another plane happened to be on the ground and its pilot rescued the injured, making two flights to get all to a small jungle hospital where they eventually recovered.

There are many people who find it difficult to keep their hands off the controls. And the crashes continue. I sympathize with the frightened

passenger, for I have a way of doing exactly the same thing in my spiritual journey. Thinking God has lost control or has ceased to care, I panic and try to take over and run things my way. It never works. Even the Lord Jesus had to submit to His Father's flight plan.

Not My will, but Yours be done.

Things may seem mighty awkward—or even scary—but we have to be willing to leave the controls in the hands of the Pilot.

It's the only way to fly.

MOUNTAIN WAVE DEPRESSION

Flying from New York to Washington in a twin-engine Beechcraft, I was tuned to Air Traffic control when I heard a pilot report over Lancaster. He was on the same route, flying northbound at 7,000 feet, a thousand feet below me. In a shaky voice, he asked New York Center for clearance to land at Lancaster Airport.

"I can't maintain my altitude," he said.

New York cleared him to land at Lancaster and asked what was the problem.

"I really don't know," he replied. "I'm getting full RPM and manifold pressure but the airplane keeps sinking. I can't keep it in the air. Must have engine trouble." Then he switched frequencies and that's all I heard from him.

Twenty minutes later, as I approached Lancaster, *my* airplane started to settle. Airspeed dropped off from 160 knots to 110 knots. I increased power to climb settings. It still settled. Engine instruments checked okay, but I was fighting to hold the plane in the air. Then I remembered the other pilot had reported the same conditions. Weird!

As I struggled at the controls, something filtered back to me from my background reading. An expression. *Mountain wave depression.* I had felt the effects of downdrafts in my mountain flying experience over the Andes of South America. But this was different. The winds were out of the west at 40 knots. I was just east of the Allegheny Mountains and the wind coming over the range was causing a huge depression area, not a momentary downdraft. It was like flying through a waterfall of wind.

Realizing this, I just stayed with it for the next 35 miles, fighting through the constant down pressures. Even with increased power I was barely able to hold the airplane in the air. Sooner or later, I believed I would break through.

Approaching Westminster, I suddenly started getting the reverse effects—*updrafts*. There was a tremendous, irresistible lift in the air. I reduced power 'way back, yet even so, my airspeed climbed over 200 knots and I could hardly keep the plane level. Risers were everywhere. I thought of that fellow on the ground back in Lancaster, nervously checking his engine. If only he had stayed with it a little longer, he would have passed beyond the influence of mountain wave depression.

Sound familiar? If you're like me, the analogy holds true for day-to-day living. I often find it difficult to hold a level course. The updrafts and downdrafts seem so unpredictable and sometimes come so close together. I'm encouraged by Paul, who had been through the depressions and then wrote back to say, "And let us not get tired of doing what is right, for after a while we will reap a harvest of blessing if we don't get discouraged and give up" (Galatians 6:9 TLB).

A VOICE IN THE STORM

The controller's voice from Houston Center was calm.

"We understand," he said. "One engine has failed. We have you on radar. Montgomery County Airport is 45 minutes southeast of your position. Would you like vectors?"

For the last half hour I had been enjoying the bright Texas sky as we cruised high above an overcast. Below us, rain and fog blanketed the ground between Dallas and our destination, Houston. Then, BANG! One engine on the Cessna sputtered and stopped. The dead prop on my right looked strange and ominous. I could still fly—one of the joys of twin engines—but I was not overly ecstatic about making a single-engine approach into an unknown airport in weather that had the ducks walking.

I glanced over at my two passengers. They were staring, transfixed, at the motionless propeller.

"We'll soon be on the ground at another airport," I said, in a weak effort to allay their anxieties. But who was around to comfort me? I reached for the mike and soon the reassuring voice of the Houston controller filled the cabin.

"Okay, Houston," I responded, "I'm with you. Requesting vectors to Montgomery Airport."

"Turn left," he said. "Heading 110 degrees. Descend to 4,000 feet."

I followed his directions implicitly, trying to keep the airplane trim and level at the same time. At 4,000 we entered the clouds, flying blind through the mist and rain.

"Descend to 3,000 and turn right five degrees," the steady voice instructed.

"Descend to 2,000 and turn left five degrees. . . . Now turn right 30 degrees and descend to 1,500 feet."

As we dipped into the rainclouds, I could barely see the tip of my wing. But I knew he knew where I was. That was enough. I didn't know his name. I had never seen his face. But I knew I could trust him. I had no other choice—unless I wanted to try and make it on my own.

Suddenly we broke out of the clouds and there it was: a mile of wet asphalt glistening in the rain. I'd never known asphalt to look so beautiful.

I'd been more than willing to entrust my life to a faceless voice speaking complex directions through the fog. Touching down, I thought of another voice. Calm, patient, ever present when over the years blinding mists have thrown carefully wrought plans into chaos. His voice.

Did I really trust that voice? As much as I trusted the stranger in Houston? Would I be willing to follow exacting instructions when I couldn't see any farther than the end of my nose?

Good questions. Questions which have to be answered...on a regular basis...like every morning.

Though you have not seen him, you love him; and even though you do not see him now, you believe in him and are filled with an inexpressible and glorious joy (1 Peter 1:8 NIV).

EXIT, THE SWASHBUCKLER

Humility comes hard for pilots. Even Christian pilots. There is something about getting behind the controls of a plane that makes a man feel, well, proud. The old caricature of the swaggering pilot with leather jacket, goggles and scarf fits most of us more than we care to admit.

Spiritual pride—the kind that goeth before a fall—snares even the best. In fact, believing you are worthy to be counted among the best is sure evidence you've already fallen.

I keep remembering the smirk on the face of one of our Peru pilots when he sauntered into the hangar following a long, hard trip over the jungle. Dropping his flight bag, he boasted, "In four days I have traveled more miles than the apostle Paul in all his missionary journeys."

A seasoned missionary in the hangar never looked up from his packing as he replied: "Yes, but did you accomplish as much?"

Would you like to know an effective anti-toxin for a case of pride poisoning? Get yourself in a position where, if God doesn't take over, you're bound to fail. That was the way I felt when I started making plans to fly a new Cessna 402 across the Pacific to Papua, New Guinea. Even having another experienced pilot like Ken Wiggers along as my copilot didn't ease the humble feeling I experienced every time I looked at those charts representing 8,000 miles of open sea. I immediately purchased two more books on prayer. When you file a flight plan from Oakland to Honolulu, you put "Glory" as your alternate destination.

By the time I was wheels up, I was all "prayed up." In fact, I was three weeks ahead in my devotions. This was one time I was determined to give God all the glory.

Just before we left I got a telegram from a good friend who's also a retired executive of Northrup Institute of Technology, my alma mater:

AS YOU LEAVE THE SHORE LINE SATURDAY
CONTINUING WEST COMMA I KNOW THAT OF THOSE
FIFTY FOUR THOUSAND ANGELS OF MATTHEW
TWENTY SIX FIFTY THREE COMMA EACH HAVING THE
POWER SHOWN BY THE ONE IN SECOND KINGS
NINETEEN THIRTY FIVE COMMA AT LEAST ONE HAS
ORDERS TO FLY RIGHT WINGMAN WITH YOU AND
AUTHORITY TO SUMMON A WHOLE FORMATION OR
EVEN A SQUADRON ACCORDING TO WHAT
MANEUVERS THE ENEMY MAKES PERIOD SO JUST
WATCH YOUR LORAN AND REJOICE PERIOD PRAISE
THE LORD

And God performed miracles on that trip. The engines ran perfectly. Even with an extra ton of fuel, the Cessna soared over the waves like a tireless gull. And when we spotted Hawaii after seven hours of dead reckoning, most of it at night, Ken and I both shouted, "Praise the Lord!"

On the next leg we had to deal with five typhoons. At one point the Lord opened a hole in the clouds just in time for us to see an island whose radio beacon had blown down in the typhoon. The flyboys could call it skill if they wanted, but I say it was God's grace that got us there.

However, after we arrived in New Guinea, a strange thing began to happen. I found myself enjoying all the congratulations, the "oh's" and the "ah's." Outwardly I was still giving God the credit, but inwardly I was accepting the praise and claiming it for myself. It's easy to get proud once you're safely on the ground.

But God had a way of dealing with that, too. The next morning I

climbed into the right seat to check out one of the pilots who would fly the 402. Just seconds into the takeoff run the right engine failed. It stopped dead. I chopped power and hit the brakes. We aborted the takeoff without incident and, using the one good engine, gingerly taxied back to the hangar. There the mechanic found that a part of the engine had seized, causing the failure.

I broke out in a cold sweat. Why had it run perfectly halfway around the world, only to fail just then? I don't know. But I do know this: It was time for the old swashbuckler to stash his scarf and goggles. From now on, God gets *all* the glory—in the air and on the ground.

THE PEOPLE GOD USES

It's strange, the people God uses.

A large church had invited me as their special guest so they could present an airplane as a gift to JAARS. It was a Bible-believing church, filled with scrubbed-faced fundamentalists—the kind I like to be around. I was the main speaker for the Sunday morning service—a real VIP.

During Sunday school a friend introduced me to a beautiful black woman who, learning I was to speak, was visiting the church for the first time. I immediately recognized her, although we had never met. She was Josephine Makil, a Wycliffe translator, home on furlough from Vietnam.

Some months before, she and her family had been ambushed on a lonely Vietnam road. She and her three children had watched in horror as her husband, and the fourth child he was holding in his arms, were murdered in cold blood. She is one of God's special people.

That morning, before I spoke, I introduced Josephine, asking her and the children to stand. She gave a brief but powerful testimony, closing by saying, "I can testify that God's ways are perfect and His grace is sufficient."

The words burned deep in my heart. I wanted to remove my shoes, so hallowed was the ground as I stood beside her. It took me long moments before I could speak. I couldn't get the lump out of my throat.

After the service people flocked around me, shaking my hand and patting my back. During the adulation I happened to look to one side. There stood Josephine and the children. Alone. In fact, the people were deliberately avoiding her. She was black.

I could hardly restrain my anger. I wanted to rush through that magnificent building, overturning the pews and shouting, "Keep your money. Keep your handshakes. Keep your airplane. It goes up as a stench before God."

But I didn't. Perhaps I was too much the coward. I did break from the group and go to Josephine. We chatted, but she said nothing about her rejection. She reacted to those church people the same way she reacted to those who murdered her husband—with love and forgiveness.

These people found it strange that God would use a black person like Josephine. I, in turn, find it strange that God would use people like those in that church—yet their gift has been a blessing to the Kingdom.

But then, I am sure some folks find it strange that God would use a fellow like me.

Josephine is right. Love is the only way to react. For all our sakes, we must leave judgment to God.

OVERBOARD!

A lady wrote to JAARS recently, asking to be put on our mailing list for "that new publication." She wasn't sure of the name but she thought it might be "Overboard."

Not bad. The name of the publication may actually be *Beyond*, but the call of God *is* for His people to go "overboard" as He directs.

My wife, Nancy, thought I had gone over the edge the night a friend phoned from California. He said he knew where we could buy a $50,000 Helio Courier for $27,500. But we needed to act immediately.

We had a "new plane" account on our books, but it was $15.83 in the red. I ordered the plane anyway. No doubt about it—it was an "overboard" kind of thing to do. Not unlike Peter's decision—who suddenly crawled over the edge of his fishing boat, planted his feet solidly on a passing wave, and started striding. Today that plane is paid for, doing duty on the mission field.

Our plan to put seven helicopters in operation within three years also sounded a little overboard. We lacked the equipment, personnel, funds and technical expertise for such a project. But we decided to go ahead anyway. Step by step, we experienced a series of miracles.

In a surplus depot in Pennsylvania, our man Jim Baptista spotted 16 metal engine containers used by the military to ship new engines. Since we'd been having trouble with our old wooden crates, Jim asked if we could have those metal ones. "You can have all 16," the man said. Looking closer, Jim discovered each container had inside it a spare engine, just the type used in our Hiller helicopters. Just like that God had supplied 16 spare helicopter engines!

Jim got more than he asked for—or even dreamed. Kind of reminds me how the apostle Paul liked to describe his Lord:

Now to him who is able to do immeasurably more than all we ask or imagine, according to his power that is at work within us.

That's overboard!

CARING ENOUGH TO CRY

Last week in my office, in the middle of a meeting with three businessmen, I began to cry. I still get embarrassed thinking about it.

A contractor from Philadelphia had flown down to spend the day at the JAARS Center here in Waxhaw. With him were two business friends who are interested in missions. We ate lunch, toured the Center and then returned to my office. Pulling out a file, I began reading to them excerpts from cases illustrating JAARS' involvement in recent mercy flights: a snakebite victim to the hospital in Peru . . . a doctor to an Indian village in Ecuador to stop an epidemic . . . relief to landslide victims in Colombia. . . .

Then I came across the case of an Indian girl named Rita in western Brazil. That touched it off. I still don't know what happened to me, but all of a sudden I began to weep. All choked up, I blushed like a schoolgirl. Fortunately, my business friends were very kind. They didn't laugh. I quickly changed the subject to aircraft operating costs, fuel consumption, range, engine overhaul time and other safe subjects in which we were interested.

I don't know—maybe they would have cried, too, if they'd known more about Rita. She'd been carried in from the jungle to the home of two single women Wycliffe translators. The moment they saw her they knew she could not live without prompt medical attention. One, a nurse, examined Rita. Finding her to be severely anemic, desperately ill with malaria and five months pregnant, she sent a radio message to the center at Porto Velho, requesting an emergency flight.

A pilot and an aviation mechanic flew out in a Cessna 206 and soon Rita was in the maternity hospital in Porto Velho. The doctors discovered her system was laced with deadly parasites and the battle was on to save her life. Men and women at the Wycliffe Center put aside busy schedules to provide around-the-clock nursing care. Many gave blood. When Rita experienced a severe reaction to a blood transfusion and the doctors said she was dying, everyone at the Center dropped what they were doing and gathered for prayer. Once again her life was spared. The hospital staff expressed amazement that so many people could love one poor, illiterate Indian woman.

I can't tell you why I cried over the report. Maybe it was the fact that Rita was so remote in that endless jungle, seemingly without help. Maybe it was because all JAARS had to do was send a plane and fly her to a hospital. Or it may have been the expense. The flight which saved Rita's life cost only $62.10. Or perhaps it was the fact that she accepted Christ in the hospital and went back not only healed, but transformed. I don't know. But something got to me and suddenly I began to cry right in front of those businessmen.

But then . . . why should I be ashamed to cry? Jesus wept. Nehemiah cried when he heard the report on the sad state of Jerusalem. And the reports I'm getting from around the world are certainly every bit as grim. God said we should go forth weeping if we are to be productive for Him. Our Lord is looking for men who care enough to cry.

If we don't, who will?

ON LOSING AND WINNING

The idea of "giving up" never appeals to us masculine types. We prefer the pull-yourself-up-by-your-bootstraps method, the blood-sweat-and-tears approach to life.

This brings to mind R. G. LeTourneau's little Piper Tri-Pacer. The incident occurred in the late 1950's on a jungle airstrip in the foothills of the Andes. There were four big men in the plane; it was a simple case of too much weight and not enough horsepower. Staggering off the end of the mountain strip, the Piper settled into the middle of a swirling jungle river, and flipped over.

The men quickly scrambled out of the plane and began swimming frantically toward shore, only 50 yards away. But the current was much too strong. Before they had fought 10 yards toward shore, they had been swept a quarter mile downstream. Death seemed imminent.

Totally exhausted, the first man finally gave up. But as his body went limp and his feet began to settle, they touched the bottom of the riverbed. To his amazement and joy, the river, which was sweeping them towards their death, *was only 30 inches deep*. Standing tall in the water he shouted to his struggling companions to stop swimming and put their feet down.

Rejoicing, but red-faced, all four men waded safely to shore.

I've done that so often it hurts to think about it. Only God knows how much my arms and legs ache from the futile exercise of trying to stay afloat in shallow water. It's like flying white-knuckled all through life.

Again and again I have been forced to give up. Each time my masculinity takes another blow. But each time the words of my Lord are stenciled on the back walls of my mind just that much clearer. It is

possible to struggle doggedly and lose everything. It is also possible to lose your life and, in the process, really find it.

A QUESTION OF FOCUS

One of the most difficult lessons to teach new pilots about landing on short, hazardous airstrips is to keep their eyes on the good part of the strip, rather than on the hazard. The natural tendency is to concentrate on the obstacle, the danger, that thing he is trying to avoid. But experience teaches us that a pilot who keeps his eye on the hazard will sooner or later hit it dead center.

If he keeps looking at the ditch at the side of the strip, inevitably he will run into it. If he focuses on the stump near the roll-out area, he'll likely bang his prop against it. The experienced pilot focuses his attention solidly on the track he wants the plane to follow, keeping the hazards in his peripheral vision only.

Pilots aren't the only ones who wrestle with this problem of focus. Anyone who majors on minors, who constantly talks about his problems, who always fears the worst or who habitually points out reasons why a plan of action won't work, will get precisely what he is trying to avoid. The Bible says a man is what he thinks. And poor Job indicated what he had been thinking about all along when he said, "For the thing which I greatly feared is come upon me."

Take demons and evil spirits. They're very real hazards. But get over-concerned about them and pretty soon they'll be all over you like a swarm of bees. The wise man focuses on Jesus Christ.

And what about those dangerous doctrinal differences looming up at the end of the strip as you try to take off? Concentrate on division and you'll wind up in the middle of a split. But focus on unity, on the things that unite rather than the things that divide, and you'll clear those obstacles with room to spare.

On my first assignment as a JAARS pilot in Peru, I was dispatched to fly three businessmen to a mountain town high in the Andes. The men had previously flown with some of our older, more experienced pilots, and were apprehensive about being piloted by a 22-year-old who was busy plotting his course on a wrinkled old map.

As I loaded their baggage, they stood to one side, talking in anxious tones. Finally one of them asked, "Captain, how long have you flown in Peru?"

"About a year," I answered.

They were increasingly nervous.

"Captain, are you sure you know where all the mountain ridges and peaks are between here and Tingo Maria?"

"No, sir," I answered. "But I know where they're not. And that's the course we're going to fly."

They looked at each other, smiled and climbed aboard.

There are many dangers on each side. But Jesus has gone before and prepared the way. I know it sounds simplistic, but all we have to do is focus on Him and pretty soon we'll be wheels up, and climbing on course.

THE R&R FORMULA

Something happens to me when I lose my pen. I become animalistic.

"All right, who stole my pen. . .? What do you mean 'you borrowed it'? You *stole* it . . .! That's the problem with you kids. No respect for other people's property."

I have probably learned more about myself in that two-minute period following the discovery that my pen is missing than at any other time in my life. And it is not very nice.

In that brief moment of supreme indignation I am fully able to justify divorce, brutality, mental cruelty and even public ridicule. After all, how do you teach your wife and children proper standards of conduct if you don't take a stand on a thing? If a wife is capable of stealing a man's pen to write out a shopping list, where will she stop? What remains sacred?

A friend of mine has developed a rather intimidating formula to measure Christian maturity. Maturity, he says, can be measured by the time it takes to move from *Reaction* to *Recovery*.

He calls it the R & R Formula.

The next time someone steals your pen—or drives a nail through your hand—see how long it takes from Reaction to Recovery. It'll tell you something about yourself. I know people who are still reacting to things which happened 40 years ago. They've *never* recovered. Most likely, they never will.

"You are only young once," said a dry-witted sage, "but you can be immature for a lifetime."

Not long ago I had a good opportunity to put the R & R Formula through the acid test. Next to my pen, my most sacred possession is a well-worn, pocket-size diary notebook. It's a 5⅜" by 3⅝" life saver. Everything I know is recorded in that tattered binder. Everything. Dates, addresses, phone numbers, sermon notes, quotes, 25 years of experiences, expense accounts. The little book is priceless. It is also a crutch.

Thus, on my approach to the Philadelphia airport when I reached into my pocket and found it gone...I went into Reaction. I last remembered having it in a phone booth at Washington National Airport. My whole world shuddered to a stop.

In the moments that followed I hit ever possible emotion: despair, frustration, anger, hate self, hate God, hate National Airport, hate the phone company.

But Reaction lasted only one minute 48 seconds, and suddenly I was into Recovery—praising God. Not bad. Two years ago the nausea would have lasted three days.

"Okay, God," I said aloud, "I'm wiped out. Ground zero. All my good stuff is gone. Now it's just me and your Holy Spirit." The more I thought about that, the better it got. Until I was genuinely *glad* the stupid book was gone.

A week later, a little package arrived in the mail. Inside was my notebook. And a note.

Dear Mr. May:

We located this notebook at Gate 16 at Washington National Airport. After a glance at its contents I was sure it was a treasured article that must be returned promptly. I did a little checking and here you are.

> Sincerely,
> Bob Walters
> Customer Services
> Allegheny Airlines

P.S. As a deacon in the Christian church I know how much these things mean and I feel honored to be able to help a man of God like yourself!

Wow! From zero to full speed in five seconds.
"By the way, Sweetheart, I seem to have misplaced my pen."

JUST ME, GOD AND THE NIGHT

There are occasional moments in life when God gets my absolute attention. Like when the engine quits on takeoff at 800 feet over a busy city. Or the fuel tank runs dry. Or ice forms on the wings faster than you can measure. Or you run out of runway and experience at the same time.

Recently I was taking off from Charlotte airport in a single engine Bellanca. It was a rainy, foggy night. Ceiling was 300 feet, visibility less than a mile. Departing Runway 5, the controller cleared me to 3,000 feet and told me to turn to a 180 degree heading. As I was climbing to altitude and turning south, the lights on the instrument panel suddenly went dim. I glanced at the amp meter. It was showing 45 amps discharge. The alternator had failed and I had lost all electrical power. Faintly, just before the radio faded out completely, I heard the controller say, "Seven Four Romeo you have just faded off my radar screen."

I quickly turned off everything electrical. I needed to save whatever juice there was left in the battery to lower my landing gear—presuming I ever found the airport in that soup.

I was alone in the darkness. No radio. No navigation signals. No lights. No contact with the ground. Lost in the rain and clouds over a busy airport.

My three passengers, dear friends, giants in the faith, loving associates—could not help me. I wasn't afraid. No child of God needs to fear, regardless how horrible the situation. No, it was a different kind of emotion. Loneliness. I was alone. Cut off from all I depended upon. Just me, God, and the darkness.

A friend of mine says God sends periods of loneliness to show us our true condition. When the props fall, the masks come off, all the supports give way—it is then we find out who we really are. And, more important, who He is.

There was enough battery left to get one radio working. I established contact with the tower, who vectored me back to Charlotte airport. By keeping the radio off most of the time, and using no lights, I was able to get the gear down and have enough juice left to use the ILS navigation.

We broke out of the clouds at 300 feet and there was that beautiful runway stretching before me.

Back on the ground I taxied to the hangar and cut the engine. There wasn't enough charge left in the battery to re-start. The short in the alternator had drained everything except what we needed to get back on the ground.

We praised the Lord and joked about the situation, but the reflections of that loneliness linger on. Perhaps we are made to be lonely. Maybe this is what Augustine had in mind when he made that statement about our souls being restless until they find their rest "in Thee."

I wonder if Augustine came up with that one on a rainy night after his alternator failed.

OF THERMOSTATS AND THERMOMETERS

Recently Dave Wike, Eastern Airline pilot, and I were flying a JAARS Helio down V-93 en route from Hampton, New Hampshire, to Philadelphia. The weather was marginal. Freezing level was 8,000 feet, right where we had been cleared to fly.

As Dave flew I kept my eye on the outside air temperature (OAT) gauge—which is nothing more than an old-fashioned thermometer. A change of one or two degrees could mean the difference between wings and prop covered with ice or smooth sailing.

As the ice began to build up I reached for the mike and requested a change of altitude from New York Center. Another five minutes at 8,000 feet would have been disastrous.

"What we need," I shouted to Dave as we dropped down to warmer air at 6,000 feet, "is a thermostat out there, not just a thermometer."

Thermometers measure the environment. Thermostats change it. Our house has a thermostat. It measures, reacts, and brings change. It makes our house comfortable.

There seem to be a lot of thermometers in the Kingdom these days. It's easy to get a reading on everything from the charismatics to the Catholics. Everyone seems to have an opinion. Sometimes I think the church is in danger of paralysis by analysis.

Rare are the thermostat people. Those who are not content with simply measuring, but are in the business of bringing change. Those who can cool down an explosive situation or build a fire under a cold church.

Recently a nearby church renovated its building. When they put up the new steeple they left off the cross and installed a weathervane. Weathervanes, like thermometers, only measure the environment. Crosses change things.

There is nothing wrong with measuring and evaluating. Every thermostat has a built-in thermometer. But the need in the Kingdom today is for men who will do more than analyze. The cry is for men who will take an uncomfortable situation and change it to meet needs and glorify God.

Otherwise, we have no choice but to request a change of flight plan to a lower altitude. And that's no way to climb on course!